SHOULD WE HAVE CELL PHONES IN CLASS?

BY RAYMIE DAVIS

Please visit our website, www.garethstevens.com. For a free color catalog of all our high-quality books, call toll free 1-800-542-2595 or fax 1-877-542-2596.

Library of Congress Cataloging-in-Publication Data

Names: Davis, Raymie, author.
Title: Should we have cell phones in class? / by Raymie Davis.
Description: New York : Gareth Stevens Publishing, [2023] | Series: What do you think? | Includes index. | Audience: Grades 2-3
Identifiers: LCCN 2021045097 (print) | LCCN 2021045098 (ebook) | ISBN 9781538278758 (Paperback) | ISBN 9781538278772 (Library Binding) | ISBN 9781538278765 (Set) | ISBN 9781538278789 (eBook)
Subjects: LCSH: Education–Effect of technological innovations on–United States. | Educational technology–United States. | Telephone in education–United States. | Cell phones–United States. | Classroom management–United States.
Classification: LCC LB1028.3 .D2879 2023 (print) | LCC LB1028.3 (ebook) | DDC 371.330973–dc23/eng/20211129
LC record available at https://lccn.loc.gov/2021045097
LC ebook record available at https://lccn.loc.gov/2021045098

First Edition

Portions of this work were originally authored by Lorraine Harrison and published as *Should Cell Phones Be Allowed in Classrooms?*. All new material in this edition authored by Raymie Davis.

Published in 2023 by
Gareth Stevens Publishing
29 East 21st Street
New York, NY 10010

Copyright © 2023 Gareth Stevens Publishing

Editor: Caitie McAneney
Designer: Michael Flynn

Photo credits: Cover, p. 1 Liderina/Shutterstock.com; back cover and series background MYMNY/Shutterstock.com; p. 5 Roman Samborskyi/Shutterstock.com; p. 7 Oksana Kuzmina/Shutterstock.com; p. 8 Yalcin Sonat/Shutterstock.com; p. 9 insta_photos/Shutterstock.com; p. 11 Syda Productions/Shutterstock.com; p. 12 (hand holding phone) cunaplus/Shutterstock.com; p. 12 (phone interface) Intellson/Shutterstock.com; p. 15 Drazen Zigic/Shuttertsock.com; p. 17 (main) Tero Vesalainen/Shutterstock.com; p. 17 (inset) New Africa/Shutterstock.com; p. 19 Monkey Business Images/Shutterstock.com; p. 21 Rido/Shutterstock.com.

All rights reserved. No part of this book may be reproduced in any form without permission in writing from the publisher, except by a reviewer.

Printed in the United States of America

Some of the images in this book illustrate individuals who are models. The depictions do not imply actual situations or events.

CPSIA compliance information: Batch #CSGS23: For further information contact Gareth Stevens, New York, New York at 1-800-542-2595.

CONTENTS

The Great Cell Phone Debate 4
School Rules 6
Helpful Tools 8
Have and Have Not 10
Look It Up! 12
A Chance to Cheat 14
Emergency! 16
Losing Focus 18
Strong Arguments 20
Glossary 22
For More Information 23
Index 24

WORDS IN THE GLOSSARY APPEAR IN BOLD TYPE THE FIRST TIME THEY ARE USED IN THE TEXT.

THE GREAT CELL PHONE DEBATE

Cell phones can be useful tools. You can use them to look up facts. You can take pictures and videos. You can keep in touch with people. Many kids use cell phones—even in school.

Some people believe cell phones are a problem in schools, though. Many people believe they shouldn't even be allowed in classrooms. Other people say that having cell phones in class helps kids learn. What do you think about the great cell phone **debate**? Let's learn about both sides.

LEARNING ABOUT BOTH SIDES CAN HELP YOU MAKE AN INFORMED DECISION.

SCHOOL RULES

Many students have cell phones. But different schools have different **policies** about their use. In some cases, cell phones are allowed and used in classrooms. In other cases, students can have cell phones in the classroom, but they must be turned off and put away.

Other schools have banned cell phones from classrooms. Students need to keep their cell phones in their lockers if they bring them to school. Using cell phones during the day is against the school rules.

HELPFUL TOOLS

Smart boards, computers, and books are all teaching tools. Some people believe cell phones are teaching tools too. Smartphones often have **apps** that can be used for many different tasks. For example, recording and **collaborating** apps can be useful.

Teachers can use educational apps on smartphones. Students can learn new things using familiar **technology**. Students can also watch educational videos and visit educational websites. Cell phones also provide them with real-world technology skills. They can learn even when they can't go to school.

Think ABOUT IT!

DURING THE COVID-19 **PANDEMIC**, 93 PERCENT OF HOUSEHOLDS WITH SCHOOL-AGED CHILDREN WERE USING "DISTANCE LEARNING." ABOUT 80 PERCENT OF THEM USED ONLINE TOOLS.

APPS LIKE ZOOM HELPED MANY KIDS LEARN FROM HOME DURING THE COVID-19 PANDEMIC.

HAVE AND HAVE NOT

Some students have cell phones. Other students don't. People who argue against cell phones in classrooms say it can leave those students out. Students who don't have a cell phone wouldn't be able to fully participate in activities that require them. It could also lead to those students being teased for being different.

There are many reasons why students might not have cell phones. Some parents aren't ready to get their children phones. Others can't buy these expensive **devices**.

LOOK IT UP!

Before cell phones, students would have to look up facts in a book or on the computer. But a cell phone is easier to carry around. It makes finding facts faster and easier. People don't have to go to a library or wait to share a computer. With a smartphone, they have all the **information** in the palm of their hand.

Some people believe smartphones can help students find useful information quickly and easily during the school day. This increases **digital literacy**.

WHAT IS DIGITAL LITERACY?

THE ABILITY TO USE TECHNOLOGY TO...

- **FIND INFORMATION** — SEARCH FOR FACTS
- **EVALUATE INFORMATION** — DECIDE IF A SOURCE CAN BE TRUSTED
- **CREATE INFORMATION** — WRITE, RECORD, OR MAKE SOMETHING
- **COMMUNICATE INFORMATION** — SHARE WHAT YOU'VE FOUND OR MADE WITH OTHERS

DIGITAL LITERACY IS ALSO ABOUT BEING SAFE AND FAIR ONLINE.

A CHANCE TO CHEAT

Some people argue that cell phones give students a chance to cheat. Students can use cell phones to help them unfairly find answers for tests, quizzes, and other schoolwork.

One of the biggest reasons why cell phones are banned from many classrooms is the opportunity for cheating. Some schools make each student turn in their cell phone before a test so they can't use it to cheat. They can pick their phone up after they're done with the test. Cheating isn't fair to your teacher, classmates, or yourself.

CELL PHONES CAN BE A LEARNING TOOL—AND A CHEATING TOOL.

EMERGENCY!

Some people argue that cell phones are great tools in emergencies. A student's parents or guardians might want to be able to get in touch with them quickly and easily. This is very important if there's an **emergency** at school.

Also, some schools send messages to cell phones if there's an emergency at or near the school. The messages tell students what to do. Banning cell phones in a classroom might keep students from getting these important messages.

IF CELL PHONES AREN'T ALLOWED IN CLASSROOMS, STUDENTS CAN'T CALL THEIR PARENTS, GUARDIANS, OR 911 IF THERE'S AN EMERGENCY.

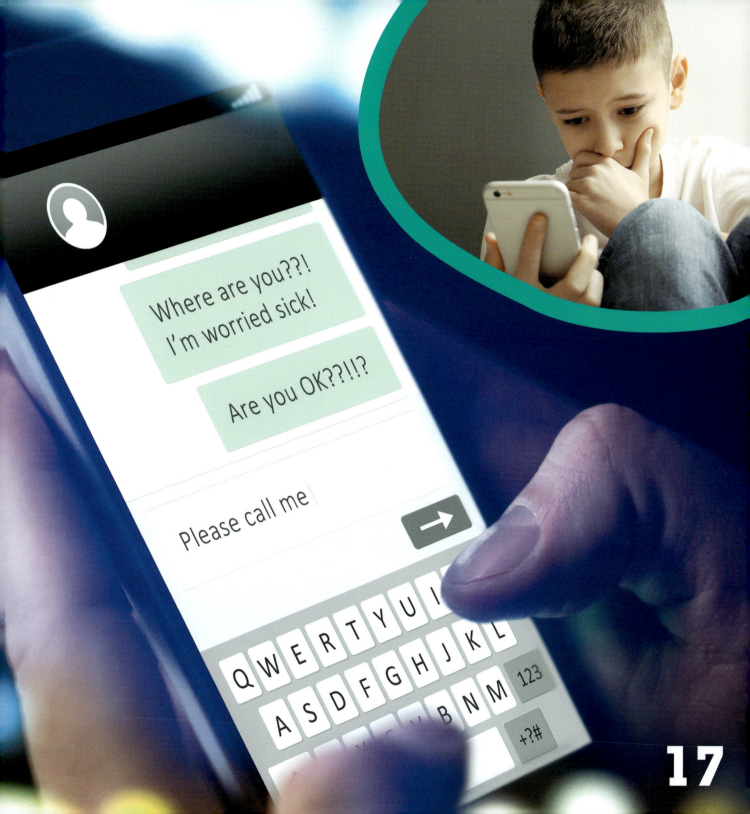

LOSING FOCUS

School is for learning. It's important for students to keep their **focus** on learning at school. But people argue that cell phones are **distractions**. They say that cell phones keep students from paying attention in class. This can lead to poor understanding or lower grades.

Cell phones can distract not only the students using them, but also other students around them. If a cell phone rings or makes another noise, it can distract people. Keeping students focused leads to higher test scores.

Think ABOUT IT!

TECHNOLOGY OVERLOAD CAN MAKE IT HARD TO FOCUS ON CLASSROOM INSTRUCTION OR CHORES.

CELL PHONES ARE IMPORTANT FOR EMERGENCIES. BUT MORE OFTEN, THEY'RE USED TO MESSAGE FRIENDS OR PLAY GAMES.

STRONG ARGUMENTS

One side of this debate sees cell phones as a problem in class. Kids can bully each other through text messages or online, which is known as cyberbullying. This can happen in the classroom if cell phones are allowed there.

The other side says that it's hard to ban cell phones because they're such a big part of life. Teachers can use cell phones to teach lessons about online safety. Both sides of the cell phone debate have strong arguments. What do you think?

GLOSSARY

app: a program that performs one of the major tasks for which a computer is used

collaborate: to work with others on a task

debate: an argument or discussion about an issue, generally between two sides

device: tool used for a certain purpose

digital literacy: the ability to use technology to find, evaluate, create, and communicate information

distraction: something that draws a person's thoughts or attention away from something else

emergency: an unexpected and often unsafe situation that calls for immediate action

focus: directing one's attention to something specific

information: knowledge or facts about something

pandemic: an outbreak of illness that affects many people in a wide area

policy: a set of rules for how something is to be done

technology: the method of using science to solve problems. Also, the tools used to solve those problems.

FOR MORE INFORMATION

BOOKS

James, Emily. *How to Be Responsible: A Question and Answer Book About Responsibility.* North Mankato, MN: Capstone Press, 2018.

Morlock, Rachael. *I Am Smart Online.* New York, NY: PowerKids Press, 2020.

Schuette, Sarah L. *Online Safety.* North Mankato, MN: Pebble Books, 2020.

WEBSITES

How to Handle An Emergency
kidshealth.org/en/kids/emergency.html#cater
Find out how you can use a cell phone in case of emergency.

Kids Rules for Online Safety
www.safekids.com/kids-rules-for-online-safety/
Read these rules for online safety before using your smartphone.

Screen Time: How Much Is Too Much?
ny.pbslearningmedia.org/resource/screen-time-above-the-noise/screen-time-above-the-noise/
Watch a video about the debate over screen time.

Publisher's note to educators and parents: Our editors have carefully reviewed these websites to ensure that they are suitable for students. Many websites change frequently, however, and we cannot guarantee that a site's future contents will continue to meet our high standards of quality and educational value. Be advised that students should be closely supervised whenever they access the internet.

INDEX

apps 8, 9

cheating 14, 15

collaborating 8

COVID-19 9

cyberbullying 20, 21

debate 4, 20, 21

digital literacy 12, 13

distance learning 9

distractions 18

emergencies 16, 19

facts 4, 12, 13

information 12, 13

online safety 20

rules 6, 7

schools 4, 6, 7, 8, 12, 16, 18

smartphones 8, 12

social media 19

Zoom 9